T0156778

The Liberal Arts in the Twenty-first Century

Exploring the Future of a Tradition

RICHARD TERRELL

iUniverse, Inc.

New York   Bloomington

iUniverse books may be ordered through booksellers or by contacting:

iUniverse
1663 Liberty Drive
Bloomington, IN 47403
www.iuniverse.com
1-800-Authors (1-800-288-4677)

ISBN: 978-1-4401-6680-8 (sc)
ISBN: 978-1-4401-6681-5 (ebook)

Printed in the United States of America

iUniverse rev. date: 08/25/2009

Dedication

To Richard Smeeth in memorium

ABSTRACT

This essay explores the thesis that the Liberal Arts tradition has been corrupted and trivialized, most importantly by disengagement from its spiritual roots. Consequently, a major task of the Liberal Arts in the 21st century will be to engage in an act of *recovery*, in which the heritage of our civilization can be affirmatively communicated to future generations. A major aspect of this recovery will see the Liberal Arts balancing the impulse toward interrogation and accusation of our civilization with renewed confidence in its virtues and unique contributions to the human condition. The role of the specifically Christian and "church-related" institution of learning will be significant for this project.

Introduction (2009)

The essay that follows was originally written in response to an invitation to faculty, from the core curriculum committee of Doane College, to offer ideas concerning the role of the liberal arts in the twenty-first century. What began as a limited summarization of my own views lead to more extended thought and reading, and eventually developed into a consideration of the issues more extensive than I, or for that matter the committee, had in mind. It became a major project for me during the summer of 2005, time that usually would have been given to painting in my studio.

Although the Doane Plan Committee seemed to have had in mind the stimulation of an on-going discussion, this did not develop to any significant degree. Indeed, the shop-talk culture of a college environment seems, ironically, to have little regard for assessing and discussing the fundamentals of what it is we are doing and why we are doing it. As refreshing a thing it may be to question our fundamental premises and expectations, it is very difficult to achieve this kind of dialogue given the normal demands of teaching, committee work, and other "ordinary" matters that press more urgently for attention.

I've decided to print an edition of the essay in the hope that it may find its way into somebody's leisure reading pursuits and stimulate some thought there, and perhaps even be useful to some open discussions that might arise. The essay is printed essentially as I wrote it in 2005, although a few references and citations have been added which represent subsequent reading and encounters with the issues. As an addendum, I have included a copy of a "last lecture" which I gave as an address to a class in Renaissance art as I neared retirement in addition to the main essay. Given that context, I believe that, despite an assessment of the lecture as somewhat "pessimistic," it will be evident that my concern is that we have built our house on ideas that contribute much of unique value to human life, that call for, and deserve, our affirmation and defense, a project that we may confidently embrace.

The immediate context from which my argument springs is my own experience at two Liberal Arts Colleges over a period of 44 years, spent at Blackburn College in Illinois and Doane College in Nebraska, both denominational, church-related institutions. To the extent that anything I have to say may have application to the broader experiences of college and university studies depends on whether I have hit upon more general, rather than merely local, tendencies. Hopefully at least some of it might be of more universal application.

INTRODUCTION (2005)

I want to commend the Doane Plan Committee for challenging the faculty to submit thoughts relating to the subject of this essay. I look forward to engaging in discussion concerning the issue of the role Liberal Arts education may play in the 21st century, and reading what others have had to say.

I do not think this subject can be approached on the basis of purely academic studies and assessment norms. When we speak of the "Liberal Arts" we are referring to a defining concept of our civilization and its educational tradition. We are referring to something that has brought a unifying thread to the consciousness of the West. One might go so far as to say the Liberal Arts tradition is a major, though not the exclusive, social element giving defining meaning to a civilization that has revolutionized human experience. So, it is not a merely "academic" subject. It goes beyond any specific concern for careers, technological acumen, or curriculum. It is, in fact, "civilizational." Any consideration of the role of the Liberal Arts in the years ahead must, or so it seems to me, look at the larger stage and the forces that might encourage or threaten the kind of inquiry we associate with the goals of liberal education.

I have given brief descriptions of the significance of the various sources informing my discussion in the bibliography. Here, I would like to call attention to a few books that stand out, and that I would recommend with special emphasis for anyone who might be interested in where I am "coming from."

George Weigel's *The Cube and the Cathedral* is a study of Europe's aversion to important wellsprings of its historic culture. He raises the issue as to why the leaders of the European Union have chosen to ignore almost 1500 years of Christian intellectual and spiritual tradition in their vision of the new Europe. Weigel sees in contemporary Europe a loss of nerve, a sense of shame concerning its own existence, and a reluctance to even believe in its own future. At the same time, the 21st century promises to see the continuing rise of a new totalitarianism, a form of despotism formed of a synthesis of radical Islam and the older, 20th century European totalitarianisms of both the Left and Right. (For a more detailed exposition of this connection see Paul Berman's *Terror and Liberalism*.) Weigel warns that Europe's problem is likely to be America's as well, that it is nothing other than a kind of civilizational suicide.

Another work of note is Alistair McGrath's *The Twilight of Atheism*. McGrath, a former atheist and Christian convert, traces the development and triumph of the spirit of religious skepticism that flows from the European "Enlightenment," while turning the tables and subjecting that tradition itself to a reverse interrogation. It is secularization, argues McGrath, that has lead to a loss of imagination and cultural courage in the West. Here, he strikes a theme similar to that pursued by Weigel. He sees the West as opening up to various spiritual outlooks, among which is a renewed openness to historic Christian premises.

In my reading, I found myself repeatedly coming across references to the name of Christopher Dawson (1899-1970), with whose work I had no prior familiarity. Dawson was a prominent British historian whose work has been neglected in recent decades. It seems to be making something of a comeback, however, in a context in which western intellectuals are considering anew the spiritual crisis of western civilization and education. That crisis is defined by a lack of unity, a fragmentation, and a pessimism that portends the West's loss of perception of its own value. Dawson's perspective, in *The Crisis of Western Education* and his other works, stresses the intrinsic relationship between Christianity and the nature of Western civilization, and the problem for the West's collective sense of itself that comes from rejecting its defining traditions. Dawson's essays on civilization and education have emerged as prophetic in view of Europe's recent attempt to separate itself from a major pillar of its own intellectual history.

The overall perspective of this paper is at odds with some favored sensibilities of the present moment, and is in tension with certain assumptions that define Doane College's self-image. However, that is the right and privilege of one who, at this stage of his career, has earned the curmudgeon's role.

Richard Terrell
Professor of Art

"In the last resort every civilization depends not on its material resources and its methods of production but on the spiritual vision of its greatest minds and on the way in which this experience in transmitted to the community by faith and tradition and education. Where unifying spiritual vision is lost—where it is no longer transmitted to the community as a whole—the civilization decays. 'Where there is no vision, the people perish.'"

—Christopher Dawson

"People without historical sense and a proper practice of tradition are so bound in the eternal now that they finally end in despair."—Walter Brueggemann

IN POSING THE QUESTION of "the task of the Liberal Arts in the twenty-first century," we are challenged first to clarify what it is we are talking about when we use the phrase "Liberal Arts." The invitation to consider this question carries with it the opportunity of setting aside the contemporary contexts in which we use the term and recover, in the interests of seeing more clearly, the ideal to which we are ostensibly committed. It is the position of this essay that the Liberal Arts ideal is itself the proper object of recovered sight, and that the Liberal Arts, once having *recovered* a sense of mission, must serve the broader recovery of a sense of virtue resident in the history and best traditions of our civilization.

The Liberal Arts provide a thread of coherence to the unfolding history of our civilization, as noted by historian Christopher Dawson:

"[T]he tradition of liberal education in Western culture is practically as old as the Confucian tradition in China and has played a similar part in forming the mind and maintaining the continuity of our civilization. For the system of classical studies or 'humane letters' . . . had its origins some twenty-four centuries ago in ancient Athens and was handed down intact from the Greek sophists to the Latin rhetoricians and grammarians and from these to the monks and clerks of the Middle Ages. These in turn handed it on to the humanists and school-masters of the Renaissance from whom it finally passed to the schools and universities of modern Europe and America."[1]

The following citation gives an effective summarization of the historic character of the "Liberal Arts," touching upon considerations of content, organization, and underlying assumptions.

"The expression *artes liberals,* used chiefly during the Middle Ages, does not mean arts as we understand the word at this present day, but those branches of knowledge which were taught in the schools of that time. They are called liberal (Lat. *liber,* free), because they serve the purpose of training the free man, in contrast with the *artes illiberales,* which are pursued for economic purposes; their aim is to prepare the student not for gaining a livelihood, but for the pursuit of science in the strict sense of the term, i.e. the combination of philosophy and theology known as scholasticism. They are seven in number and may be arranged in two groups, the first embracing grammar, rhetoric, and dialectic, in other words, the sciences of language, of oratory, and of logic, better known as the *artes sermocinales,* or language studies; the second group comprises arithmetic, geometry, astronomy, and music, i.e. the mathematico-physical disciplines, known as the

---

1   Christopher Dawson, *The Crisis of Western Education* (New York: Sheed and Ward, 1961), 6.

artes reales, or *physicae*. The first group is considered to be the elementary group, whence these branches are also called *artes triviales*, or *trivium*, i.e. a well-beaten ground like the junction of three roads, or a cross-roads open to all. Contrasted with them we find the mathematical disciplines as *artes quadriviales*, or *quadrivium*, or a road with four branches. The seven liberal arts are thus the members of a system of studies which embraces language branches as the lower, the mathematical branches as the intermediate, and science properly so called as the uppermost and terminal grade." [2]

The author of this quotation, Otto Willmann, writing in the *Catholic Encyclopedia*, acknowledges a broad background for this notion of the "Liberal Arts." As also noted by Dawson, above, Willman states that our concept has roots in ancient Greece, Rome, and Medieval Christendom. However, the author also sees that our concept of Liberal Arts also touches the traditions of the Orient as well, discovering "analogous forms as forerunners in the educational system of the ancient Orientals," in which "the science or doctrine of divine things. . .were pressed into service, four of which, viz. Phonology, grammar, exegesis, and logic, are of a linguistico-logical nature, and can thus be compared with the Trivium; while two, viz. Astronomy and metrics, belong to the domain of mathematics, and therefore to the Quadrivium. The remainder, viz. Law, ceremonial lore, legendary lore, and dogma, belong to theology." [3]

In regard to the above, we may note certain essential qualities of the concept of the "Liberal Arts."

o   Certain avenues in the pursuit of knowledge are more ***essential*** than others.

---

2   =Otto Willmann, "The Seven Liberal Arts," in *The Catholic Encylcopedia Online*. Accessed at   http://www.newadvent.org/cathen/01760a.htm
3   Ibid.

o   *The pursuit of knowledge is valuable for its own sake*. This is strongly implied by the contrast between the *artes liberales* (the "training of the freeman," the pursuit of "science in the strict sense of the term") and the *artes illiberales* (training "for economic purposes" and "preparation for a livelihood.")

o   The concept of the Liberal Arts, in its western evolution as well as its Oriental analogies, is strongly rooted in a sense of transcendent realities and *pursuit of the sacred*. These roots inform even the modern, secularized culture of the west.

We see here the outlines of discussions of recent years concerning tensions between "fundamental knowledge," "cultural literacy," and the increasing attention paid, in the halls of academe, to "career development." Also we note, in respect to the third principle, the increased secularization of education, even in the environments of so-called "Church-related" or "Christian" liberal arts colleges.

This discussion is not all that new. Willmann, in the article cited, calls attention to Hugo of St. Victor (d. 1141) as one who offered positive affirmations of "erudition," or knowledge of all sorts, even things normally counted as trivial (in *"Eruditio Didascalici"*), a tendency that grew through the centuries of the Renaissance so that by the 17th century "erudition" had begun to eat up, Pack-Man style, the *artes*. This, Willmann states, marked the developing corruption of the older ideal of "Liberal Arts."

Still, Hugo did not reduce all knowledge to an "equal opportunity" status. He continued to hold that "among all the departments of knowledge the ancients assigned seven to be studied by beginners, because they found in them a higher value than in the others, so that whoever has thoroughly mastered them can afterwards master the rest rather by research and practice than by the teacher's oral instruction [anticipating our more current notion of *continuing education*]. They are, as it were, the best tools, the fittest portals through which the way to philosophic truth is opened to our intellect. Hence the names *trivium* and *quadrivium*, because here "the robust mind progresses as if upon roads or paths to the secrets of wisdom."

A major turning point comes with Amos Comenius (d.1671), who in his *Orbis Pictus* writes scornfully of "those liberal arts so much talked of" (as in "so called" liberal arts), and in *Magna Didactica* claims that students trained in encyclopedic knowledge ("erudition") "rise to greater height." For Willmann, Comenius's thought marks a point at which undergraduate studies take on an increasingly encyclopedic character leading to the academic department system "in which the various subjects are treated simultaneously with little or no reference to their gradation," eventually resulting in an approach in which "the principle of the *Artes* is finally surrendered." [4]

Suggestions that the Liberal Arts ideal has lost its way were made in 1970 in a series of lectures by intellectual historian Robert Nisbet, delivered to the John Dewey Society in Chicago, and later published in book form under the title *The Degradation of the Academic Dogma* (Basic Books, 1971). I will interact with Nesbit's thesis with considerable emphasis, as I regard it as a seminal work that anticipates some of the more noisily celebrated critiques of higher academe that have appeared since, such as E.D. Hirsch's *Cultural Literacy* or Alan Bloom's *Closing of the American Mind.* Given the date of Nisbet's book, it seems to be prescient. I found it interesting and compelling when I first read it in the 1970s, and find it even moreso in light of my own observations and participation in the professional life of academe since 1965.

Early in his argument, Nisbet offers a telling reminder to those of us in academe who might be inclined to see colleges and universities as crucial to the pursuit of knowledge. "The university," writes Nisbet, "is only one of a number of possible ways of meeting the problem faced by all societies: *that of keeping*

---

4   Ibid.

alive the springs and the contexts of the knowledge necessary to survival; and also that of transmitting, through whatever channels, this knowledge from generation to generation."(emphasis mine)[5] I have added emphasis to Nisbet's text, because the two goals cited by Nisbet will play a role as my own discussion unfolds. The main point that Nisbet wants to make, however, in the context of his own discussion, is to remind us that "we err seriously if we make knowledge, its discovery and its dissemination even at the highest levels, synonymous with the university." [6]

That reminder is well taken. However, the Doane Plan Committee's invitation places our concerns strictly within the life of an institution of higher learning. Nevertheless, it is certainly worth keeping in mind that should colleges and universities fail in their responsibilities, other venues exist or can be formed outside them to accomplish the fundamental work of sustaining the intellectual foundations upon which our society and civilization are built.

What does Nisbet mean by his reference to "academic dogma?" How has it been lost, or "degraded?"

Nisbet draws a relationship between the concept of "dogma," as it applies specifically to religion, and the broader arena of civilization. A dogma is something that "seems good" (from the Greek *dokein*), and no society is free of dogma—nor a religious group, secular society, nor the enterprise of education represented by the college and university system. Although the concept of "dogma" is perceived in our day with almost knee-jerk negativity, it is not true that dogmas are beyond the possibility of rational examination, or that their truth cannot be demonstrated through reason, logic, or evidence.

What *is* true of dogmas, however, is that they are privileged from the kind of inquiry that would demand rational or empirical verification each and every time they are invoked, for neither

---

5   Robert Nisbet, *The Degradation of the Academic Dogma* (New York: Basic Books, 1971), 17.

6   Ibid., 18.

societies or individuals can exist without a common recognition of beliefs widely regarded as good or right without necessity of constant scrutiny." If every individual were to be "compelled to demonstrate and re-demonstrate to his own satisfaction each of the propositions he lives by, his obligation would never end," his strength exhausted and his action stymied by the necessity of preparatory demonstration.[7]

> "No community, no organization, no institution, then, can exist for long without dogma; without a belief or set of beliefs so deeply and widely held that it is more or less exempt from ordinary demands that its goodness or rightness be demonstrable at any given moment."[8]

What, then, is the academic dogma that has been degraded? Nisbet offers a strikingly simple premise: the academic dogma is that *knowledge is important.* Then, he adds an emphasis that invites melancholy reflection on the culture of liberal arts colleges prior to the innovative fad of "careerism" that flooded the academic culture in the mid 1970s: "Just that. Not 'relevant' knowledge; not 'practical' knowledge; not the kind of knowledge that enables one to wield power, achieve success, or influence others. *Knowledge!"* [9]

Nisbet notes that the academic dogma recognized that knowledge has *rank.* That is, we recognize that some pursuits are more foundational than others. "Knowledge is thought of as stratified, with some types manifestly superior to others at any given point in time. One of the prime functions of the academic community has always been assessment through criteria peculiar to itself of the relative worths of knowledge."[10] This "aristocratic" nature of knowledge (as pursued in the academic culture) has,

---

7   Ibid., 23.
8   Ibid., 24.
9   Ibid., 24.
10   Ibid., 25.

through the centuries, created an inverse relationship between the prestige of knowledge and its practicality and obvious utility. For Nisbet, this "aristocracy," is seen most clearly in the Humanities, which "because their historic status, [reflect] better than any of the 'useful' disciplines, the profound role of dogma." [11]

We may take up an objection here. Is Nisbet not vulnerable to the criticism that is sometimes leveled at the Liberal Arts by skeptics of their value, that they constitute so much "ivory tower intellectualism" and, in the final analysis, are good *for* nothing?

Nisbet counters this assertion by pointing out that no matter how "creative or sterile, leaden or buoyant" the essence of the academic dogma may have been, it always made a significant contribution to the development of the mind and personal character. Indeed, from the earliest developments in the university curriculum down to the present time, the university and its academic dogma were predicated upon a powerful sense of service to society. A very real social and moral development took place, a fact for which there is vast testimony in the forms of memoirs, autobiographies, and countless other records. [12]

What may we say of the present condition of Liberal Arts education? If we say that, in fact, the academic dogma that has sustained the Liberal Arts approach has become "degraded," (and in this I am in agreement with Nisbet's thesis), what is the nature of this degradation? What forms does it take?

It bears noting, to begin with, that Nisbet does *not* readily associate the historic academic dogma, or the classical pursuit of curriculum, with "Liberal Arts." In fact, he writes scornfully of "so-called liberal arts" programs to the extent that what is meant by the term is some sort of cloistered, meditative, allegedly "pure" pursuit set apart from any concerns for the social world outside the university. He also looks askance at the experimental "liberal arts" programs that evolved in the 1950s emphasizing curricula spotted with "interdisciplinary" courses. Although I tend to

11   Ibid., 27.
12   Ibid., 36.

disagree with Nisbet on this latter point, having experienced the interdisciplinary core Humanities course at Illinois Wesleyan University in 1959-60, and in my judgment much to my benefit, I am in overall accord with his analysis of how the degradation of academe has evolved in the past and how it continues today.

The degradation has a number of elements which I will address in turn. Whereas Nisbet's thesis will continue to influence the following discussion, I will add my own observations that are informed by what I have seen in the decades succeeding his book (1971) and, where appropriate, apply these observations to Doane College specifically.

At the time he wrote, Nisbet put his finger on something that would become more prevalent in the years following his book. He warned against what he calls "project research," or "the higher capitalism," which began to appear in the 1940s and 1950s. He sees the gradual dilution and loss of soul in the academic dogma in the embrace of *academic entrepreneurism*. The availability of *money*, and lots of it, from government and foundation sources, began to erode the cogency of the curriculum. Nisbet cites many examples in the realm of major universities, but here let me cite two major developments that had major impact at Doane College and other Liberal Arts institutions: Career Development and "Leadership" programs.

There is no faculty member at the college today who was around at the time who will not remember the changed atmosphere at Doane following a presidential announcement in the mid 70s that "career education" would, from thenceforth, become the guiding mantra of a Doane education. Substantial publicity was garnered for the school's new outlook, as if all that had gone before had neglected the useful application of a college education, that *now*, at last, graduates would know where they were going after graduation and why. Pressure was put on faculty and students alike to get a handle on the future, to know precisely what the student would "do" upon graduation. Students were even subjected to inquisitorial meetings with faculty on a day in which a moratorium on classes was held (sort of an administration-inspired "Stop Day"), the students having to justify their studies in relation to a clear future goal (in truth, none of us knew what we were supposed to be doing). "Goals" became the theme of new student orientation. Soon, faculty began to encounter a different set of questions from prospective students and their parents as they made inquiry into a Doane education, and outside observers began to refer to Doane as "the jobs school."

Initially, we all thought this to be a distinctive initiative peculiar to Doane (it was promoted as such, as if Doane were unique in this departure), but it soon proved to be a general trend across the entire country, fed by money from outside academe but which was targeted for purposes of turning the academic enterprise to goals envisioned elsewhere, by other people, and for whatever purposes they may have had. By the mid eighties, studies of American academe were showing the radical effects of this trend, revealing that, whereas in the 1960s almost 80% of college students cited *framing a view or philosophy of life* as a primary motivation for their studies, as opposed to a mere 20% seeking a specific professional career, that orientation had now been effectively reversed.

For the past decade or so, Doane has embraced the mantra of "Leadership." Although promoted as a locally conceived initiative, this perception soon gave way to the realization that "leadership" was being encouraged nationwide on campuses in a trend fed by substantial amounts of foundation money. Indeed, it looked to perceptive observers that someone, somewhere, and for whatever purpose, had deemed it necessary for colleges to emphasize the development of "leaders" and the study of "leadership," as if one did not study leadership by, say, reading *Henry IV* or *Richard III*, or studying the World War II speeches of Winston Churchill in a course in History, or as if the Liberal Arts had failed, in the past, to produce effective leaders in the arenas of culture, business, or politics. Clearly, if we apply Nisbet's thesis, academic institutions will turn down no money made available to them, and will bend in whatever direction necessary to get it.

There is probably no emphasis of the college today that so clearly draws a contrast between the older academic dogma and the "degraded" academe of our time than the so-called "leadership" emphasis. Aside from the fact that reference to Doane as "the leadership college" is pretentious (as if we are the only college around that produces graduates with leadership qualities), it burdens the curriculum itself with an implicit sense that something in a course of study is lacking if there is not some special "leadership component," elements added into the courses through the ever-present availability of grant money to make the addition. The Leadership program also illustrates a point strongly emphasized by Nisbet, that the degraded state of college and university studies is characterized by attempts to achieve, through direct programmatic emphases, goals or outcomes *that have always been the product of Liberal education*, although previously achieved as a natural *by-product* of the pursuit of knowledge, implicit and indirect but nevertheless real.

"Has it not been said, from the beginning of the history of the university, that from the proper study of the disciplines individuals acquire strengths not previously possessed? Did not the British government, through all the greatness of the Empire, go to Oxford and Cambridge for the men of leadership, moral stamina, and imagination it wanted? . . . . We can state the matter this way: under the academic dogma, the knowledge that was accumulated and transmitted in the university was, in a real sense, its own reason for being. No other reason had to be manufactured. But at one and the same time there was widespread belief that students, in their assiduous and disciplined pursuit of this knowledge, would inevitably sharpen intellectual powers and discover mental energies not previously known. . . . Mind, character, and individuality, all of these are clearly beneficiaries of the pursuit of knowledge, no matter how abstruse or remote from present-day concerns this knowledge may be." [13]

A moment's reflection on this contrast explains much about contemporary "assessment" plans. If desired results in student character (leadership skills, "appreciation" levels, etc.) are left to emerge naturally from the process of pursuing knowledge, then it goes without saying that the pseudo-scientific assessment of such matters is veritably impossible and a great waste of time. Only if such qualities are thought of as the products of consciously conceived plans monitored by ever-watchful guides can "assessment" make much sense or justify the detoured faculty energies needed to give it the illusion of credibility.

In a closely related development, Nisbet's critique raises the question as to whether college and university studies have evolved into what we know as a "tail wagging the dog" scenario. He identifies what he calls the *"cult of individuality,"* by which he means the diversion of attention from the pursuit of learning in legitimate academic disciplines to tasks having to do with the personal needs of the individual student. He asserts that, in the interests of meeting the social and psychological needs of students, bogus liberal arts ("so called") programs have diluted academic pursuits into curricula of "snippets" serving the extra-academic needs for "social tolerance," "adaptation to a changing world," and so forth. More recent developments in the "assessment" cult sees the assigning of primary emphasis on personal "outcomes," with actual subject matter and intellectual substance serving as mere points-of-departure, as if almost anything will do.

Nisbet was surely onto something in 1971 that has since burgeoned into pseudo-intellectual emphases on "self esteem" and "multicultural sensibilities," both of which were still over the horizon when he wrote. Although the first of these has been substantially discredited from an intellectual perspective, it still

13   Ibid., 116-117

functions to undermine teaching and learning, intimidating decisions as to what may or may not be said in a classroom situation or other public educational venue, to say nothing of the assigning of grades. The second—"multiculturalism"—is so ever-present today that it has, arguably, been raised up as a new, substitute academic dogma in its own right. It is, in fact, the new "establishment." Professors today question its premises almost at the peril of their jobs. Certainly reputations or collegial relationships risk negative consequences for a failure to "get on board."

Pseudo-disciplines and therapy goals, however, provide us with a point-of-departure for the contemplation of the question before us, and can help focus our consideration of the future and destiny of college and university studies. Let us keep in mind the responsibilities faced by all societies, and the role that college/university studies may play in fostering them, cited toward the beginning of this essay, that of *"keeping alive the springs and the contexts of the knowledge necessary to survival; and also that of transmitting, through whatever channels, this knowledge from generation to generation."*

As demonstrated by the history of the Liberal Arts idea, the knowledge "necessary to survival" is rooted in the recognition of principles deemed to be transcendent and sacred. Even the anti-clerical mentality of the Enlightenment did not completely lose sight of a vision of human liberty and human rights as being rooted in a transcendent, divine source. That the political and educational institutions of the West seem to have forgotten these origins of our common intellectual life is evidenced in the European Union's proposed constitution, which excludes all mention of Europe's past Christian orientation, and in the progressively secularized environments of American liberal arts colleges over the past half-century, most of which were themselves founded as expressions of theological vision. As to the "Christophobia" of European intellectuals and politicians, as well as dominant trends in higher education, the reader is referred to a number of recent books which address the central role of Christianity in the foundations of our civilization.[14] Here, let us consider the premise that, in looking ahead, one of the tasks of the Liberal Arts in the 21st century is one of *recovery*—specifically the recovery of the *sacred dimensions of knowledge* and the recognition that some pursuits are more foundational than others.

What is generally meant, today, by a "Liberal Arts" experience? Clearly, the weight here is carried by the notion of so-called "distribution requirements," or what Robert Nisbet criticized as "snippets." Anybody who has ever labored on a "general education" committee knows the difficulty of defining the opposite thereof, the idea of "core" curriculum. Not only is the "core" extremely difficult to define to everyone's satisfaction (a difficulty certainly deepened by the exponential explosion of knowledge and factual data in modern life), the idea of a core curriculum is offensive and dangerous to departmental interests that govern the internal politics of institutions. The classical idea of the Liberal Arts, grounded in the sacred character of knowledge, was governed by the premise that some pursuits were more *essential* than others, more centered as to their significance for the task of "*keeping alive the springs and the contexts of the knowledge necessary to survival; and also that of transmitting, through whatever channels, this knowledge from generation to generation.*"

While educational policy commitments can present two dominant paths to decadence—an ossified canonization

---

14   See: Thomas Cahill, *How The Irish Saved Civilization* (New York: Doubleday, 1995); Vincent Carroll and David Shiflett, *Christianity On Trial:Arguments Against Anti-Religious Bigotry* (San Francisco: Encounter Books, 2002); Gerald J. Russello, ed., *Christianity and European Culture: Selections from the Work of Christopher Dawson* (Washington, D.C., The Catholic University of America Press, 1998); Alvin J. Schmidt, *How Christianity Changed the World* (Grand Rapids: Zondervan Publishing Company, 2003); Rodney Stark, *For The Glory of God* (Princeton:Princeton University Press, 2003); George Weigel, *The Cube and the Cathedral* (New York: Basic Books, 2005); Thomas E. Woods, Jr., *How The Catholic Church Built Western Civilization* (Washington, D.C., Regnery, 2005); David Bentley Hart, *Atheist Delusions: The Christian Revolution and Its Fashionable Enemies* (New Haven, Yale University, 2009).

of authoritative works on the one hand, or an anarchic, "democratized" pursuit on the other, the trend has been toward the latter rather than the former, as is evidenced by Doane's freshman LAS program. Looking over this program gives the impression that the substance and content of a curriculum "introducing the Liberal Arts" to new students is largely irrelevant. Almost any subject will do, and is equally serviceable to the goal of fostering student "behaviorial objectives." One wonders, however, how we can have a program of "introduction to the Liberal Arts" in which no unifying exposure, applicable to all the students, is given to works of foundational influence to our civilization, or in which the only common thread is a book representing a single individual's memoirs and sentimental reflections, chosen largely on the basis of compatibility with "multiculturalist" objectives.

Nevertheless, the idea of the "Liberal Arts" constitutes a tradition of great antiquity which has endured for many centuries. It is not formless, and is an objective historical phenomenon. Why would an introduction to the "Liberal Arts" concept be so reticent to guide students into a sense of its historic content and development, its *essential elements?* Here, Arthur Bestor's exhortations of many years ago seem relevant, through which he called his colleagues to recognize that Liberal Arts education

"must begin with a courageous assertion that all the various subjects and disciplines in the curriculum are *not* of equal value. Some disciplines are fundamental, in the sense that they represent essential ways of thinking, which can be generalized and applied to a wide range of intellectual problems. Other disciplines, though equal in intellectual potency, are somewhat less central to the purposes of liberal education, either because they can be studied only after the fundamental disciplines are mastered, or because they represent highly specialized intellectual techniques, restricted in their range of applicability. Other courses in the modern curriculum do not represent disciplines at all, but offer professional preparation, or training in mechanical skills, or helpful hints on vocational and personal matters. Still other courses, alas, offer nothing at all, save collections of more or less interesting facts, opinions, or fallacies."[15]

I bring attention to this in order to speculate that the secularization of education has lead in the direction of trivialization and confusion, for it is the secular spirit that eschews recognition of hierarchies and ultimately reduces ideas to the lowest common denominator of authority. In the final analysis it undermines the goals of "*keeping alive the springs and the contexts of the knowledge necessary to survival,*" a goal that requires evaluation and decision-making as to what is, after all, of essence, and "*that of transmitting, through whatever channels, this knowledge from generation to generation,*" a goal that gives special place to issues of cultural heritage.

Some will surely suggest that I am overstating the case here. Besides, is not secularization the *necessary* stance of modern education, the inevitable outgrowth of "natural" intellectual forces evolving over many years? Is it not merely a matter of making some adjustments to necessary forces of progress, which have appropriately marginalized transcendent and religiously grounded worldviews? My response is "no," for the trivialization of curriculum is inherently related to the trivialization of knowledge, as a reality related to *truth,* and this erosion itself has deepened as our civilization has passed through the stages of "post-Christian" to "Modern" to "post-Modern," each step of the way making the reality of truth more problematic and thus, as a natural consequence, creating a sense that knowledge is merely instrumental rather than an entry into what Russell Kirk

---

15   Arthur Bestor, *Educational Wastelands* (Urbana: University of Illinois Press, 1953; Second Edition 1985), 162-163

has called "the permanent things."[16] Can anyone deny that the concept of "truth" as an energizing principle in higher education is less compelling and credible today than the more seductive mantras of "information" and "data?"

Nor is it clear that secularization is the natural and necessary context for liberal education. Recent historical and sociological research reveals that, far from secularism's "natural" evolution and influence in western institutions, it is more accurately understood as the outgrowth of consciously pursued agendas. If so, then it has been more of a choice, rather than a necessary consequence of overwhelming, "naturally evolved" intellectual forces.[17] And if that is true, then it is a choice that can reasonably be challenged and put to contemporary assessment with no danger to anyone's intellectual integrity. Given this, there is every reason to say that one of the tasks of those concerned for the Liberal Arts in the 21st century will be a reconsideration of the intellectual premises and assumptions upon which the enterprise has come to rest, an act of *recovery* of the Liberal Arts in a sacred tradition that has room for transcendent truths. This is certainly a credible project for "Christian" or "church-related" institutions.

The skeptic may ask, "but what 'truths' are you talking about?" I am willing to let the cards fall where they may, given a renewed commitment to, and recognition of, the *premise* that Truth (capital "T" and lower-case) is real, and that our civilizational heritage has something to teach us about it, that *it is worth knowing.* At the very least, it is worth pursuing as a question to be taken seriously, as a way of rediscovering a sense of unity and integration to liberal education. As Christopher Dawson exhorted his readers in 1961,

---

16   See Russell Kirk, *Enemies of the Permanent Things* (New Rochelle, New York:Arlington House, 1969).

17   See Christian Smith, ed., *The Secular Revolution: Power, Interests, and Conflict in the Secularization of American Public Life* (Berkeley: University of California Press, 2003), especially Smith's essay "Secularizing American Higher Education: The Case of Early American Sociology," 97-159.

"Heaven forbid that we should try to solve our educational problems . . . by imposing a compulsory… ideology on the teacher and the scientist! But we cannot avoid this evil by sitting back and allowing higher education to degenerate into a chaos of competing specialisms without any guidance for the student except the urgent practical necessity of finding a job and making a living as his education is finished. This combination of utilitarianism and specialism is not only fatal to the idea of a liberal education, it is also one of the main causes of the intellectual disintegration of modern Western culture under the aggressive threat of [totalitarianism]."[18]

Let us briefly consider the record of educational progress prior to the late 19th and early 20th century secular transformations of American institutions of learning. It is simply an uncontestable fact that for most of its history, "higher education…has been an enterprise pursued in a religious context and under religious influences."[19] Most scholarship in the Middle Ages was carried out by monks in their monasteries and later in cathedral schools and universities. As to the university itself, it owes its existence to Christianity, for the Church showed a vital interest in the preservation and pursuit of knowledge. The very names of medieval universities fostered in the context of Christendom still command our attentions with authority. Rodney Stark presents the Christian influence on higher education in the Middle Ages:

> The university was a Christian invention that evolved from cathedral schools established to train monks and priests. . . . Oxford and Cambridge were founded around 1200, and then came a flood of new institutions [at] Toulouse, Orléans, Naples, Salamanca, Seville, Lisbon,

---

18   Christopher Dawson, *The Crisis of Western Education*, 132-133.
19   Christian Smith, *The Secular Revolution*, 97.

Grenoble, Padua, Rome, Perugia, Pisa, Modena, Florence, Praque, Cracow, Vienna, Heidelberg, Cologne, Ofen, Erfurt, Leipzig, and Rostock. . . . It is estimated that during the first 150 years of their existence, European universities enrolled approximately 750,000 students in an era when the population of London was never more than 35,000. . . . [Nor were they] primarily concerned with imparting the received wisdom. Rather, just as is the case today, faculty gained fame and invitations to join faculties elsewhere by *innovation.* The results were entirely predictable: factions formed and reformed; new schools of thought abounded; controversy became the dominant fact of scholarly life. In a world over which One True Church claimed exclusive doctrinal authority, the spirit of free inquiry cultivated in the universities made theology the *revolutionary* discipline. . . ."[20]

Nor should it escape our memory that the great abundance of colleges and universities in the United States, from Harvard to humble rural colleges, trace their origins to Christian people and purposes. Harvard's historic motto grounds that institution's existence and purpose in Christ: *Christo et Ecclesiae,* the words surrounding the Latin word *Veritas.* The motto of Frieburg University in Germany has Biblical roots: *Die Wahrheit wirt euch freimachen* (The Truth Shall Make You Free). Doane College's original motto was *We Build on Christ,* a statement that evokes profound meditation on the possibility of knowing "the treasures of wisdom and knowledge." (Colossians 2:3) It survives as a relic of the past, receiving annual lip service in the singing of the *Doane Hymn* at commencement proceedings, but for all meaningful purposes it has passed away under preference for slogans like "Challenge Yourself™," which evokes little more

---

20   Rodney Stark, *For the Glory of God: How Monotheism Led to Reformations, Science, Witch-Hunts, and the End of Slavery* (Princeton University Press, 2003), 62-63.

than self-centeredness, or, more recently, the innocuous "call" for "*Impact*."

In a matter of mere decades, beginning in the later 19th century, this sense of the sacred dimension of the pursuit of knowledge (and truth) had been effectively shelved. Although the popularly accepted narrative of this change sees institutions of higher learning as overcoming "hide-bound" theological roots under the sway of new knowledge and science, this narrative itself is eroding under new scholarship. Christian Smith observes that "careful studies have shown that colleges were much more diverse and adaptive than the standard account allow[s]" and that research into the activities of church-related, liberal arts colleges reveals that faculty "did engage in progressive academic research that moved scientific knowledge forward." Further, "the nineteenth-century Christian college system was not nearly as moribund or repressive as the standard account has led us to believe." [21]

Indeed, classic works defining the so-called antagonism between Christianity and modern, scientific understanding, most notably John William Draper's *History of the Conflict Between Religion and Science* (1874) and Cornell President Andrew Dickson White's narrative *A History of the Warfare of Science with Theology* (1876), are now seen to be biased polemics, written in the conscious interests of secularizing American intellectual life.[22] The claims set forth in these famous and influential books, although largely discredited by historians of science, still live on in the thinking of academics and in popular culture, and most recently underwrite the "historical" elements of the phenomenal best-selling fiction works of Dan Brown, *The Da Vinci Code* and *Angels and Demons*. Yet, appearing under the cultural radar,

---

21   Ibid., 100.

22   Ibid., 121-123; 135, 144. Stark, a leading sociologist of religion, in his various citations of White's work, forcefully exposes   the mistakes, distortions, and dishonesty of the Princeton president's classic. See also Alistair McGrath, *The Twilight of   Atheism* (New York: Doubleday, 2004), 85-87.

in recent years and largely out of view of many academics, the whole popular narrative of Christianity's "war against science and reason" has met with many challenges. David Bently Hart's perspective is representative of these challenges, and is explored in depth in his book *Atheist Delusions: the Christian Revolution and Its Fashionable Enemies.*

> "[R]espectable historians of science today have no use for either of these books and are well aware that the supposed war between Christian theology and Western science is mythology of the purest water. Unhappily a myth can be discredited and still be devoutly believed."[23]

Given the history of creative educational energies in a Christian context that have fostered Liberal Arts education, and the sustained, centuries-long tradition of such, *is it not at least reasonable to question whether any genuine concept of the Liberal Arts can long survive if cut off from roots that acknowledge the transcendent and the sacred?* For clearly, the present-day secularized context for the pursuit of the Liberal Arts is an historical anomaly. Of deeper significance, however, is the degree to which the transformation to a secular mode of life has failed the purposes of liberal education, narrowing its *perspectives* while ever increasing its subjects, obscuring its *vision*, and ultimately, as in the case of Europe, demanding a severing of major root lines of nourishment.

Why, though, should we be so concerned about our own civilization? What's so great about *it*? These questions, which animate certain extremes of "multicultural studies" today, lie at the heart of what George Weigel cites as the civilizational suicide of the west, seen most clearly in Europe's conscious denial of a major life stream of its achievements, and a widespread sense of guilt about its very existence. To the extent that Europe and

---

23   David Bentley Hart, *Atheist Delusions: The Christian Revolution and Its Fashionable Enemies* (New Haven: Yale University   Press, 2009), 56.

America share much in common, culturally, it is problematic whether a tradition such as the Liberal Arts can be sustained in a context of our own intellectual self-flagellation and chic shame that seeks to *define* western civilization by its worst failings, and in the process nullify its real achievements and essential contributions to the human condition.

Multiculturalism, beyond its harmless fostering of awareness of non-western and/or minority achievements, weakens Liberal Arts studies through its massaging of a sense of grievance and resentment of the past and a lowering of visibility of common humanity.[24] The destructive nature of "multiculturalism" for the academic enterprise is seen not only in various incidents of the propagation of academic fraud,[25] but in its uncritical acceptance in colleges as a necessary and viable perspective, to say nothing of the heavy-handed manner in which its acceptance is enforced on faculty who may, from time to time, gather the courage to voice their skepticism. Ironically, in departing from the older academic dogma, colleges find themselves in bondage to newer dogmas supported not by historical moorings but by mere ideology and the exercise of power and position in academic environments.

These issues influence more than just the recovery of the "religious" base of Liberal Arts education, specifically the biblical, Judeo-Christian bloodstream, but invite a renewed perspective on the issue of why and how we need to "transmit the knowledge

---

24   For critical perspectives on multiculturalism in educational practice, see *Chronicles: A Magazine of American Culture* (September, 1995), especially Charles L. King, "Multiculturalism in Theory and Practice," 23-24;

25   A celebrated recent case is that of Ward Churchill, author of bogus scholarship and a dishonest claim of American Indian ancestry, a professor at the University of Colorado. Other notorious cases of bogus scholarship occur in race-based studies, such as the Stolen Legacy theories that classical Greek civilization was a literal theft of African culture, or the fraudulent Latin American autobiography *I, Rigoberta Menchu: An Indian Woman in Guatemala* (defended by the *Chronicle of Higher Education* even after its fraudulent character was exposed in 1999.) On these matters and other cases of multiculturalist erosion of academic integrity, see Mary Lefkowitz, *Not Out of Africa* (New York: Basic Books, 1996)

necessary for survival" to succeeding generations, knowledge that comes from classical Greco-Roman and Enlightenment sources as well. I would question, however, that such a responsibility can be carried out by individuals and institutions that have, at the core of their outlook, a sense of grinding guilt about our own civilization, or who are ready to marginalize its achievements in the interests of an ideologically driven "shame game." For, as George Washington University's Jonathan Chaves states, "If we repudiate a grounding in the West under the influence of a radical egalitarian ideology which holds all cultures to be of equal value and importance, and of equal interest to us, we will undermine the very ground we stand on." [26]

As a professor of East Asian Languages, Chaves is no parochial advocate of western *hubris,* but he points to the inherently curious character of western civilization that has, in the past, motivated western scholars to examine and learn about civilizations beyond the West while challenging the multiculturalist premise that all such interest was merely in the service of colonialism. He writes:

> "My plea [is] this: let us require the students to receive a solid grounding in the great classics of the West and in the entire Western heritage. Our own university and the whole system of higher education of which it forms a part is a product of the West. The academic freedom which allows us to explore the complete range of knowledge is a product of the West. The very enterprise of systematically and dispassionately studying another civilization, while empathetically entering into its aesthetic sensibility, historically has emerged only in the West."

Chaves's comments were first stated as an appeal to the General Requirements debate at George Washington University, and argue that the nature of western civilization and its intellectual life will

---

26 Jonathan Chaves, "When West Meets East," *Chronicles* (September, 1995), 13-16.

lead, quite naturally, to the exploration of the wider arenas of human experience without the artificialities of "multicultural" goals grafted onto the educational enterprise, for "such study is and has been for centuries part of the noble endeavor of seeking knowledge as an end in itself."[27] In a similar vein, Paul Gagnon reminds us of the expansive education involved in the singular attention to a subject like American History. "The plain fact is that American history is not intelligible, and we are not intelligible to ourselves, without a firm grasp of the life and ideas of the ancient world, of Judaism and Christianity, of Islam and Christendom in the Middle Ages, of feudalism, of the Renaissance and the Reformation, of the English Revolution and the Enlightenment. . . . The blood of American students ran in men and women working the soil of Burgundy and the Ukraine, or China and Africa, before the Normans set out on their conquests."[28]

Liberal Arts education, then, has a distinct and peculiar responsibility to *western* civilization. It is, after all, *ours*, and it provides the context for the very existence of the Liberal Arts to begin with. As such it is our specific responsibility to preserve, transmit, and defend it. But note how shocking such a proposal sounds in today's context, given the intimidating nature of multiculturalist and post-modern dogmas. Indeed, how anachronous, even rude, seems the claim made by G.K. Chesterton: "When all is said, if there were nothing in the world but what was said and done and written and built in the lands lying round the Mediterranean, it would still be in all the most vital and valuable things the world in which we live." [29]

Some may assert that I am advocating a chauvinistic purpose for the Liberal Arts. No, I am merely advocating that higher education undertake what is a central purpose of any healthy

---

27   Ibid.

28   Paul Gagnon, "Why Study History?" in *The Atlantic* (Volume 262, No. 5: November, 1988): 46-47.

29   G.K. Chesterton, *The Everlasting Man* (San Francisco: Ignatius Press, 1993. Originally published 1925 by Dodd, Mead and Company), 78.

society that has enough self-respect to acknowledge its right to exist—the communication of its distinct heritage to succeeding generations, without apology. In saying this, I do not mean to say that this civilization was, or is perfect or even close to perfection, or even necessarily *better* that some others. There is much in the European and Anglo-American heritage that we might lament. The point, however, is that there are distinctive virtues within that heritage that allow us to honestly confront and study those failings, hopefully learning from them. This freedom is itself one of the greatest influences of Christendom upon the larger western tradition—a version of the Hebrew tradition of "prophetic" vision, where renewal may be invoked through the voices that see social realities without illusion.

We have been through a period of intense scrutiny and vigorous interrogation of the West and Christendom, wrought by voices within and without. Now, in the century ahead, I suggest that it is the right thing to see again, with clearer vision, what are real virtues in this civilization, recognizing that they bring real substantial grace and beauty to human life, and that these virtues are worthy of being sustained in our remembrance and even our advocacy. What I am suggesting here is analogous to a comment regarding iconoclastic interpretations of Winston Churchill, made by historian G.R. Elton, who insists that we err if we cannot think that there have been great individuals, despite their flaws, for surely we can see that "no matter how much better the details, often damaging, of man and career become known, he still remains, quite simply, a great man." [30] Can we not invoke the same principle in the study of our own civilization?

Christopher Dawson (1889-1970) wrote with singular passion in this vein. Not only did Dawson keenly sense a loss of perception of the West's distinctive virtues and the Christian foundations of western culture, but he noted one of the prevalent influences of secularism on education—a loss of a sense of unity

---

30   Cited by Gertrude Himmelfarb, *On Looking Into the Abyss* (New York: Alfred A. Knopf, 1994), 38.

in the pursuit of knowledge and the fragmentation of learning into disjointed and narrow specialties. Dawson was concerned to return a sense of unity and integration to college and university studies. He advocated making the study of the West a central project for liberal education, for it was foundational for understanding the modern world itself, even its significant secularization. "For it is hardly too much to say that modern civilization *is* Western civilization. There are very few forces living and moving in the modern world which have not been either developed or transformed by the influence of Western culture." Nor can consideration of the centrality of Christianity to Western civilization be overlooked or marginalized, for, remarks Dawson, "as Dr. Toynbee himself has shown, Western civilization is inseparable from Christian civilization, and the latter is the more fundamental and intelligible unit."[31]

At this point, I must plead the uncertainties of predicting the future. The very question before us assumes a certain picture of what the 21st century will be like. How can we outline the task and role of the Liberal Arts in the 21st century without knowing the context? Clearly we can't, at least *I* can't. I can only state what I believe to be urgent at this moment, given what the Liberal Arts have been, what they have become and why, and make a case for recovery on the basis that such recovery of vision will be good for learning and the intellectual and spiritual sustenance of our civilization. Nevertheless, certain realities emerging in the world over the past decades indicate the possibility of major civilizational dislocations and transformations that will call for the Liberal Arts to play an apologetic role in the intellectual defense of the west.

Here, let us consider a few anecdotes from recent history that may provide some clues to our question.

o   In June 2004, the draft constitution forming the basis for final treaty negotiation for the European Union, in

---

31   Ibid., 126-127.

presenting the roots of contemporary Europe and its commitment to democracy and human rights, while citing the classical heritage and the Enlightenment, excluded the entire 1500 year history of Christian influence on the formation of European civilization.

o In late 2004, Rocco Buttiglione, a distinguished Italian philosopher and Minister for European Affairs in the Italian government, was held unfit for service as Commissioner of Justice in the European Commission, a division of the European Parliament. The reason for this was Buttiglione's moral perspectives, formed by his Catholic faith.

o In November, 2004, a Dutch filmmaker, Theo van Gogh, was murdered in broad daylight on an Amsterdam street by a Dutch-Moroccan named Mohammed Bouyeri. Van Gogh was killed because he had produced a short film exposing the human rights abuses toward women in Islamic society. Bouyeri evidently saw his individual act as a paradigm for a larger quest—the destruction of the Netherlands itself, along with the rest of Europe and the United States. [32]

o In the summer of 2005, the acclaimed Italian journalist Oriana Fallaci was indicted by an Italian court on the initiative of Italian Muslims. Her crime was having written a book, *La Forza della Ragione* (*The Force of Reason*), in which statements allegedly "insensitive" to Islam were written.

o In July 2006, in the aftermath of Islamic jihad attacks in London, Sheikh Omar Bakri, an Islamic intellectual leader and former head of the Islamist

32 This citation and the two preceding are discussed in George Weigel, *The Cube and the Cathedral* (New York: Basic Books, 2005), 56-63; 160-161; 193.

"Al-Muhajirun" organization in Britain, confidently declared that "loyal Muslims in Britain will one day turn it, with Allah's help, into 'Islamistan.'" He also repeated statements he had made in 2001 about the "banner of Islam" flying over British landmarks and government buildings.[33] It is not unusual today to find observers of British life increasingly referring to London as "Londonistan."

In the wake of the above events, others followed which achieved more notable international attention, most infamously the international threats, property destruction, and deaths respondent to the publication of some mildly satirical cartoons of the Muslim prophet Muhammed in the Danish newspaper *Jylands-Posten*. The cultural intimidation implicit in the Islamic response has proved to be significant for the entire civilization of the west, as journalists, intellectuals, universities, and politicians in Europe and America responded to the violence with a general and resounding silence, or, invoking multiculturalist concepts of "sensitivity," opted for appeals to "understanding" rather than boldly defending open and free expression. What students and faculty would do well to understand is that an event such as the "cartoon controversy" is not merely a local matter for people living in Denmark. The issues are civilizational, as recognized by the president of the Norwegian Press Association, Per Edgar Kokkvold:

> "*Our civilization* [emphasis mine] is built on two foundations. One of them is awareness of the individual human being's absolute value independent of race, religion, and social background. The other is the freedom to think and express one's thoughts. If freedom is to have

33   See interview with Bakri at The Middle East Media Research Institute, July 12, 2006.   (http://memri.org/bin/articles.cgi?Page=archives&Area=sd& ID=SP120306)

any meaning at all, it must mean the freedom to say what others don't like to hear." [34]

All of these events, prominent or obscure as they may be to most citizens, tell us something about the role of the Liberal Arts in the 21st century. That role will be nothing less, I will suggest, than the task of keeping practices of intellectual inquiry and historical consciousness alive through the building of a regained sense of confidence in western values and practices, and that this task will itself demand of the Liberal Arts an act of *recovery* and reconsideration of essential orientation. This consideration will be contextualized by the two forces implicit in the above anecdotes. The first is historically established and has already heavily influenced the life of academe, as discussed above—the power of secularism. The other is likely to present an ongoing, long-range challenge to everything implied in the phrase "Liberal Arts" or "liberal studies"—the reality of Islamist-fascist totalitarianism and its program of jihad against the west.

Although Samuel Huntington's thesis of a coming "clash of civilizations" (1993) was highly controversial at the time he wrote it, one does not have to be committed to a particular theory of history to see that, indeed, something like that is in the air, at least in regards to the fascist elements of international Islamic jihad. Of the events cited above, the first two illuminate European "Christophobia" and rejection of the historical reality of European Christendom by the very societies that have been shaped by it. Can the West jettison its historic religious impulses without losing its culture? The others are expressive of a long-range ideological and totalitarian vision rooted in the work of

---

34   Quoted in Bruce Bawer, *Surrender: Appeasing Islam, Sacrificing Freedom* (New York, Doubleday, 2009), 57.

early 20th century theoreticians of Islamic empire,[35] catalyzed over the past decades by the Islamic Revolution in Iran and its expressions elsewhere in the form of public declarations of war against the "infidel" West (1996, 1998). However tempted we may be to think that the latter are marginal forces that will calm down through changes in U.S. foreign policy, we may be reminded that the same perception of marginality attended Europe's Christophobic denial of its intellectual and spiritual roots, and that rising energies of Islamist-fascist jihad are likely to play major roles in shaping the character of the 21st century.

Here an objection may be raised. Is this not mere alarmism? I don't think so. It is, however, to consider an alarming possibility. George Weigel's sobering analysis of Europe's declining intellectual and spiritual morale, and what it portends for America, is bracing. He calls attention to the "population meltdown" among the historic populations of Europe, and the filling of the consequent demographic vacuum by Islamic immigrants, a significant number of which have no identification with their host countries and are attracted to radical Islamist-fascism. Other observers, such as the Jewish historian Bat Ye'or, already see the emergence of a new civilization—"Eurabia"—expressing the possibility of a substantially Islamized Europe at some point in the present century. To those who would object that such a development is impossible, Weigel cites the example of the ancient Greco-Roman-Christian civilization of North Africa, which became vulnerable to Islamic armies and "disappeared into the sands,"

---

35   The origins of contemporary Islamo-fascist jihad and the relationship of its brand of totalitarianism to 20th century European utopian/totalitarian visions are explored in the excellent work of Paul Berman, *Terror and Liberalism* (New York: W.W. Norton and Company, 2003). Berman's analysis locates the premises fueling Islamist jihad in the writings of Sayyid Qutb (1906-1966), the most important theorist of contemporary Islamic Revolution. See also Robert Spencer, We Are Not Fighting Just Al Qaeda, *Human Events,* May 27, 2004, which outlines the historical, post World War I roots of present-day jihad. For an illuminating discussion of the nature and implications of Europe's diminished civilizational morale and depopulation trends see George Weigel's *The Cube and the Cathedral* (n. 32 above).

in mere decades, its cultural strength "sapped" of any energy able "to persuade itself that its civilizational accomplishment could and should be defended." [36]

No less an analyst of European affairs than Walter Laqueur has sounded the alarm over a declining Europe and its vulnerability to its burgeoning immigrant populations. He cites multiculturalist doctrine as having fostered a more tribal sensibility among immigrants, who are on the verge of becoming majority populations in a number of European cities today. Insofar as these immigrant groups foster no admiration for western values, the demographics of Europe present grave challenges to the continued viability of those values. He even entertains the possibility that Europe might become a kind of "theme park" culture, a tourist attraction dedicated to remembering a past civilization! He describes the reflections of European thinkers at the turn of the millennium in 2000: "One could only hope that the newcomers indifferent to European values or even hostile to them would gradually show more tolerance, if not enthusiasm, toward them or that multiculturalism, which has been such a disappointment, would perhaps work after all in the long run. These were not exactly strong hopes."[37]

Laqueur also warns of another challenging force that is emerging in major population centers of Europe, a thoroughgoing *non-religious* culture rooted in violence and nihilism involving resentful, angry youths of Muslim background who have, like Christian young people in the west, rejected the traditional culture and religion into which they were born. This is essentially a "barbarian" culture, fueled by street gangs. They are without ideology, embracing hip-hop aesthetics celebrating violence and even sadism. Laqueur observes that "to understand the scenes in the schools and streets of Kreuzberg and the *banlieues* [Paris

---

36 Weigel, 155

37 Walter Laqueur, *The Last Days of Europe* (New York, St. Martin's Press/ Thomas Dunn Books, 2007), 15.

suburbs], a texbook on juvenile delinquency could be more helpful than the Koran."[38]

It is likely a mistake to think that such events as those cited above will abate in the years ahead. If anything, they are likely to intensify, whatever the specific conditions of European or American politics may be, or how effective emergent "dialogical" voices prove to be.[39] As far as American Liberal Arts education is concerned, it will not have the option of narrowly defining its mission in terms of marketplace preparation, career development, technological progress, or ethnic and gender politics. It will have to take up, again, as a central task the serious issues of universal human nature and destiny as the over-riding context for educational practice.

It is doubtful that the Liberal Arts can be sustained in an atmosphere defined by a dominating negation of the traditions and heritage within which the concept was initially nourished and the fashionable, relentless interrogation of our own civilization as void of virtue. If, as radical multiculturalism asserts, the story of Western civilization is to be understood solely in terms of bias and oppression and iconoclastic interrogation, then the question becomes, as posed by Neil Postman, whether we can find any "narrative of organizing power and inspiring symbols which all citizens can identify with and draw sustenance from." If not, then do we not face a situation in which "education must become a tribal affair," with mere subcultures asserting their own stories and symbols?[40] As author Lee Harris forcefully observes, the dangers posed by a "sham and racist" multiculturalism lies in the refusal "to recognize that there are certain things on which all cultures have agreed, and chief among these is the rejection of de-civilization, that is, the rejection of those who deliberately

---

38   *Ibid.*, 45.

39   See John L. Esposito, *Unholy War: Terror in the Name of Islam* (Oxford: University Press, 2002). Esposito challenges Huntington's clash of civilizations thesis and outlines aspects of Islamic pluralism.

40   Neil Postman, *Technopoly* (New York: Vintage Books, 1993), 178.

try to undermine and subvert the level of civilization of whatever culture they are attacking. . . . For us, the only question is, whose world is ending, and whose is just beginning?" [41]

I do not wish to suggest here that the major issue for the future of our civilization will be, necessarily, terrorism. In reality, there is a possibility that acts of outright violence might diminish, in favor of a quieter form of jihad—cultural and intellectual in character. It is wise, I would affirm, to take influential voices in the Muslim world seriously, voices that are increasingly confident that, within the lifetime of today's college students, major urban areas in the West, if not larger territories, will be living under Islamic, not western, law. It is likely that western civilization and its institutions will be increasingly engaged in what Walid Phares has identified as the "war of ideas." Already we see increasing pressures from immigrant groups, scornful of western ideas and values, advocating a setting aside of western legal and moral concepts to facilitate the institution of Sharia law in their own neighborhoods or larger areas of residence. Sharia law, would, of course, allow *in western countries* punishments like public stonings, "honor killings" (now being practiced in European countries to the fearful silence of authorities), or capital punishment for apostasy (conversion from Islam to another religion).

What do these concerns mean, in terms of practical application, for curriculum in a Liberal Arts context? As a final consideration, let us focus on what may be some necessary and valuable actions in regard to the general atmosphere of the Liberal Arts college and matters of subjects and courses. Here, we may call into question some of academe's most entrenched presuppositions that have currency today. But, if the themes of *recovery of essence* and *transmission of heritage* are granted, then we might proffer the following possibilities:

o   Instead of curriculum *expansion* as the signal evidence of growth, we may consider the possible benefits

---

41   Lee Harris, *Civilization and Its Enemies* (New York: Free Press, 2004), 212

of *deleting* courses, leaving more to the intellectual initiative of students. We consider the possibility that the press to do "more and more" at some threshold undermines the power and integrity of Liberal Arts studies.

o If we recognize, as central to the concept of the Liberal Arts, that *knowledge has rank*, then we may consider anew the nature of all-college requirements. Should every discipline, or even "area of study," be represented in a general education program such as the Doane Plan?

o *Truth* may be reaffirmed as a relevant concept animating the educational environment, and the recognition of the sacred dimension of learning may be meaningfully restored. The present spirit of "postmodernism," pursued consistently, offers a death blow to any rationale for education.

o A healthy confidence in our western experience need not be seen as antithetic to critical evaluation of historic realities, recognizing that inwardly focused critique is itself part of the western tradition. However, the element of preservation and confidence toward our historic moorings is appropriate.

o The idea of the "Christian Liberal Arts College" may be strengthened[42] through a recognition of the inherent historic relationship between Christianity and the Liberal Arts. A significant civilizational role will be played by educational institutions with a theological vision.

---

42   See Michael S. Hamilton, "A Higher Education," *Christianity Today,* June 2005 (Vol. 49, No. 6): 31-35. Also Charles Habib Malik, *A Christian Critique of the University* (Downers Grove, Illinois: Intervarsity Press, 1982).

As will be evident by now, I do not believe we can address the question posed by the Doane Plan Committee through an uncritical and continuing acceptance of the familiar group of "outcomes" that have come to guide our deliberations in campus "shop talk" venues. Before we talk about the role, or task of the Liberal Arts in the 21st century, a prior and more fundamental question begs to be addressed: *What are we really talking about when we employ the concept of "Liberal Arts?"* Further, what guides our response to that question other than opinions that can embrace any trendy subject to catch the fancy of the day? It will be clear from the preceding discussion that my assumption is that something vital has been lost in our easy reference to "Liberal Arts," and that there are essential aspects that need to be recovered, and that the strength of that recovery may effectively foster the fundamental educational tasks of a healthy society—to preserve itself through the preservation of knowledge necessary to survive (indeed to foster faith in the justification of survival), and to effectively pass on that *essential* heritage to generations to come.

There are ways in which the Liberal Arts idea has been wounded and eroded by the decisions and actions of those responsible for its life. A question worth asking is whether we are not so far removed from the center of it as to prevent our nourishing it to life again.

ANNOTATED BIBLIOGRAPHY

Bruce Bawer, *Surrender: Appeasing Islam, Sacrificing Freedom* (New York: Doubleday): 2009

Bawer is a gay western journalist living in Europe who moved from the U.S. to escape its oppressive atmosphere toward homosexuals to enjoy the freer environs of Europe. There, he became alarmed at the growing oppression of free expression in the wake of European embarrassment over western values and history in the face of Muslim cultural intimidation.

Paul Berman, *Terror and Liberalism* (New York: W.W. Norton and Company): 2003

Berman's discussion relates the nature of present-day Islamist jihad to earlier, 20th century totalitarianism, and warns that the fashionable cultural iconoclasm of western intellectuals may ultimately serve to undermine liberal civilization.

Arthur Bestor, *Educational Wastelands: The Retreat from Learning in Our Public Schools* (Urbana: University of Illinois Press, 1953; Second Edition 1985)

This book is a classic critique of "progressive education" in public schools, and reveals why real educational reform is so difficult to achieve. Especially relevant to the concerns of this present paper is his chapter entitled "The Structure of Liberal Education."

Allan Bloom, *The Closing of the American Mind: How Higher Education Has Failed Democracy and Impoverished the Souls of Today's Students* (New York: Simon and Schuster): 1987

The best-selling critique of higher education of the late 80s. Bloom's ideas were criticized as "elitist," given his withering criticisms of popular culture and what he sees as higher education's compromised capitulation to trivialities and fads.

Thomas Cahill, *How The Irish Saved Civilization* (New York: Doubleday): 1995

An eye-opening discussion of the vital role played by early medieval Christian monks in the preservation and transmission of ancient knowledge and literature.

Jack Cashill, *Hoodwinked: How Intellectual Hucksters Have Hijacked American Culture* (Nashville: Nelson Current): 2005

This book is an iconoclastic work that exposes the fraudulent roots of many of the broadly accepted narratives of our cultural "story," and their unquestioning acceptance by academic and culturally "progressive" people.

Vincent Carroll and David Shiflett, *Christianity On Trial: Arguments Against Anti- Religious Bigotry* (San Francisco: Encounter Books): 2002

This book is one book in an emerging genre of Christian "cultural apologetics" works that seek to respond to the post-Enlightenment iconoclastic mentality toward Christian history and the civilization of Christendom.

G.K. Chesterton, *The Everlasting Man* (San Francisco: Ignatius Press):1993.

A classic affirmation of the power and integrity of a Christian worldview by one of the 20th century's most radical thinkers.

Christopher Dawson, *The Crisis of Western Education* (New York: Sheed and Ward): 1961

An eloquent and passionate discussion of the foundational presence of Christianity for an understanding of Western civilization, and the rationale for the study of the West in basic and higher education. There is much of interest here in the tensions between classical education and the effects of modern secularism. Dawson's central premise is that any society that disregards its spiritual foundations will collapse, no matter the level of its material well-being.

John L. Esposito, *Unholy War: Terror in the Name of Islam* (Oxford University Press): 2002.

A balanced overview of Islam's history and present situation. Esposito sees hope for the marginalization of Islamic jihad by advocates of dialogue with the West within Islam. The world's response to Jihad-inspired terrorism is a serious matter for intellectuals, academics, religious leaders, and ordinary citizens.

Oriana Fallaci, *The Rage and the Pride* (New York: Rizzoli): 2002

An internationally honored Italian journalist's passionate indictment of western cultural and political leaders for what she sees as their craven fear of defending the virtues of western civilization in the face of Islamist threats. Ironically, Fallaci, who is an atheist, is shown to be a most forceful advocate for the historic civilization of Christendom.

Lee Harris, *Civilization and Its Enemies* (New York: Free Press): 2004

Harris illuminates how civilizations organize and sustain themselves in the face of internal forces of decay and the confrontation with external enemies. A major theme is how the intellectual may become the enemy of civilization.

David Bentley Hart, *Atheist Delusions: The Christian Revolution and Its Fashionable Enemies* (New Haven: Yale University Press): 2009

Hart's work in a frontal assault on popularly embraced narratives concerning the alleged conflicts between Christian belief and reason, science, and human achievement. It is an excellent example of the burgeoning collection of "cultural apologetics" affirming the positive influences of Christianity upon our civilization while avoiding chauvinistic romanticizing.

William A. Henry III, *In Defense of Elitism* (New York: Double-day):1994

Henry offers a powerful defense of merit and achievement, and vigorous criticism of fashionable "isms" in contemporary education.

Gertrude Himmelfarb, *On Looking Into the Abyss: Untimely Thoughts on Culture and Society* (New York: Alfred A. Knopf): 1994

Valuable perspective on the moral and intellectual implications of trendy theories of deconstruction and postmodernism.

Stanley Jaki, *The Savior of Science* (Washington, D.C., Regnery Gateway): 1988

A probing discourse on the relationship between the Christian worldview and the development of modern science. The author affirms the compatibility and (as with A.N. Whitehead) intimate link between western scientific thought and practice and the premises of Judeo-Christian theism.

Russell Kirk, *Enemies of the Permanent Things* (New Rochelle, New York: Arlington House):1969

The author examines the question of what endures and why, and argues that there are transcendent virtues and truths in the world's great literature. "When the moral imagination is enriched, a people find themselves capable of great things; when it is impoverished, they cannot act effectively even for their own survival."

Walter Laqueur, *The Last Days of Europe: Epitaph For An Old Continent* (New York, St. Martins Press/Thomas Dunn Books): 2007

Laqueur offers a vivid picture of the shifting streams of optimism and pessimism concerning European civilization in the post-World War II decades. His analysis argues persuasively that the expectation of many that things are just going to remain more or less the same in the future for western society and values is highly problematic.

Mary Lefkowitz, *Not Out of Africa* (New York: Basic Books):1996

A challenge to the claims of "Afrocentrist" scholars that the classical Greek civilization was merely derivative, and based on the conscious "stealing" of African culture.

C.S. Lewis, *The Abolition of Man* (San Francisco: HarperCollins Edition): 2001. (Orig. pub. 1944)

A classic examination of the fallacies of subjectivism and

the reality of objective values. Lewis's point of departure is a critique of an English text book for British preparatory school students. He affirms a universality of human values expressed in various cultural traditions, identifying this universal tradition as the *Tao*.

Charles Habib Malik, *A Christian Critique of the University* (Downers Grove, Illinois: Intervarsity Press):1982

Malik offers a specifically Christian critique of contemporary college/university studies based on the Christian origins of the university and the Christian influence on the development of American institutions of higher education.

Alistair McGrath, *The Twilight of Atheism* (New York: Doubleday): 2004

Oxford professor exposes the development of the modern secular spirit and offers explanations on why the fashionable atheism of post-Enlightenment intellectual life is in decline. He argues that it is secularism's revealed lack of imagination that has undermined its credibility and attraction.

Robert Nisbet, *The Degradation of the Academic Dogma* (New York: Basic Books):1971

A seminal work offering critique of higher education's loss of integrity. Nisbet traces the beginnings of declining integrity in university studies to the post-World War II infusion of corporate and foundation money fostering academic entrepreneurialism. He also questions "student sensitive" practices.

Jarolav Pelikan, *Jesus Through the Centuries: His Place in the History of Culture* (New Haven: Yale University Press): 1985

Pelikan's thesis is simply stated and forcefully argued: that if you removed everything that referred to the single individual Jesus Christ from the material culture and intellectual heritage of the West, you would effectively obliterate an entire civilization from human memory.

Régine Pernoud, *Those Terrible Middle Ages! Debunking the Myths* (San Francisco: Ignatius Press): 2000

A lively polemic against the popular notion of the "Middle Ages" as a time of ignorance and stagnation. Pernoud, a French historian, challenges the popular notion that the civilization of the Renaissance was culturally superior to medieval culture.

Neil Postman, *Technopoly: The Surrender of Culture to Technology* (New York: Vintage Books): 1993

Postman argues that our confidence in technology is significantly over-rated. Human life, learning, discovery and cultural achievement are not only possible without it, but certain technologies may even dilute those possibilities.

James V. Schall, *Another Sort of Learning: Selected Contrary Essays on How Finally to Acquire an Education While Still in College or Anywhere Else* (San Francisco: Ignatius Press):1988

Various personal observations and perspectives on the limitations, questionable premises, and possibilities of formal higher education. Written by a professor at Georgetown University

Alvin J. Schmidt, *How Christianity Changed the World* (Grand Rapids: Zondervan Publishing Co.): 2003

A thematically organized treatment of the influence of Christianity on the formation of our civilization's approach to law, economics, the arts, science, and human rights.

Christian Smith, ed., *The Secular Revolution: Power, Interests, and Conflict in the Secularization of American Public Life* (Berkeley: University of California Press): 2003

Smith questions mainstream secularization theory's claim that secularization was a "natural" evolution owing to overwhelming evidences in its favor. The essays in this book show how secularism was the product of consciously pursued intellectual agendas, the special focus of which was the transformation of educational practice at all levels.

Rodney Stark, *For the Glory of God: How Monotheism Led to Reformations, Science, Witch-Hunts, and the End of Slavery* (Princeton University Press): 2003

Stark is the country's leading sociologist of religion. This book looks at history and many favored narratives concerning the influence of religious belief and practice with fresh eyes. In the process, the author disturbs the orthodoxies of academe's dominant "progressive" thought.

George Weigel, *The Cube and the Cathedral* (New York: Basic Books): 2005

A startling thesis that Europe is presently in the process of committing civilizational suicide through population decline and a denial of the spiritual roots of the west. He sees the long-range effects of this as not being merely Europe's problem, but eventually America's as well.

Thomas E. Woods, Jr., *How The Catholic Church Built Western Civilization* (Washington D.C., Regnery): 2005

An affirmation of the Catholic church's positive and shaping role in western civilization. Similar to Alvin Schmidt's book (above), but from an unabashedly Catholic perspective. A good antidote to the fashionable anti-Catholicism of post-Enlightenment intellectual life.

PERIODICALS AND WEBSITE ARTICLES

Jonathan Chaves, "When West Meets East," *Chronicles: A Magazine of American Culture* (September, 1995)

Paul Gagnon, "Why Study History?" *The Atlantic* (November, 1988) Volume 262, No. 5

Michael S. Hamilton, "A Higher Education," *Christianity Today,* (June 2005) Vol. 49, No. 6

Lee Harris, "The Future of Tradition," *Policy Review* (June & July, 2005), No. 131.

Charles L. King, "Multiculturalism in Theory and Practice," *Chronicles: A Magazine of American Culture* (September, 1995)

Robert Spencer, "We Are Not Fighting Just Al Qaeda," *Human Events* (May 27, 2004)

Otto Willmann, "The Seven Liberal Arts," in The Catholic Encylcopedia Online. Accessed at http://www.newadvent.org/cathen/01760a.htm

"So What Is This All About, Really?" (Or, "Why Bother?")

Richard Terrell, to Art 205 Visual Communications in History

May 8, 2009

Author's Note: *The following presentation was given to students in an art history course, and as indicated in the text, it follows a "last lecture" concept. An administrative colleague who read it remarked that she thought it sounded a bit "pessimistic about civilization." For me, the concepts of "pessimism" and "optimism" are relatively meaningless. What matters, I think, is reality, and for me there are two major realities that underlie what I chose to say here. First, societies and civilizations are under no guarantee as to their continued existence, and secondly, most students (and I think faculty as well) today operate on the assumption that, come what may, things are going to stay pretty much the same, in fundamental ways, as they are now, or that a society in which freedom of expression is supported with legal protections is a more-or-less "normal" situation. I believe that contemporary realities challenge that assumption, and that liberal education is tasked with the responsibility of awakening young people to an awareness of that challenge. To do so, it seems to me, is not an act of "pessimism" at all, but an act that can only be predicated on a foundation of hope. If not, then why say anything at all? This is not a time for rosey muticulturalist platitudes. We are the inheritors of humanizing values and truths that emerged through centuries of struggle and immense courage. But nothing is a mere given, and my words to the students sought to convey this. Upon retrospect, it does seem to me that the lecture is best understood in relation to the longer, preceding essay expressing the thoughts which inform it. Therefore, it makes sense to me to bring them together here.*

As this is our last regular class meeting, I thought I would engage in an exercise which is commonly designated, in academic culture, as a "last lecture." The premise is, if you had to give an address, a final address, to the learning community, what would you say. As this is, literally, my last lecture at Doane College, I'll go ahead with it. What I would like to do is put the course of study we've been through in a larger, and summarized "civilizational" context

The first consideration is the significance of what you have studied over the course of this semester, and there are four points I would stress here:

a. Works of art embody a civilization's soul. Over time, a tradition forms that constitutes a *heritage*. Every generation within the stream of that heritage faces the question as to what will be done with it. Healthy civilizations and societies embrace it, seek to refine and add to it worthily, protect it, defend it, and pass it on.

b. The character of works of art (their intellectual and spiritual vision, scope, ambition, and physical presence) is directly related to the larger matrix of ideas, principles, premises, that nourish the mental ethos (the intellectual "soil") from which they grow.

c. Civilizations arise, flourish, and decline according to a dynamic of cultural strength or weakness. Civilizational coherence tends to lead to a cultural product that is ambitious, expressing confidence in that society's will to exist and the sense of the rightness of its existence. It is, in this respect, no mere accident that the Renaissance saw its initial flourishing in the city of Florence, or that the classical period of Greece's "Golden Age" was manifest in Athens. Or that the people of the middle ages built mathematically and technologically astonishing architectural edifices that remain among the world's man-made wonders.

d.   Civilizations decline and vanish through an erosion of confidence, a process that may be long and drawn out or caused by the crises of encounter with a civilization that is stronger, more accomplished, or perhaps just more militant.

Secondly, the studies of this course present you with a basis for assessing a question that, I believe, poses itself today with a gathering urgency: *If you had to defend the civilization that is yours, would you know enough about it, would you have enough appreciation for its achievements, to engage in its intellectual defense and, if need be, its physical defense?*

This question is now, and I believe will be increasingly urgent, to your generation. This course has presented but one aspect of a grander whole, centered on artistic product, but the question is really much larger than a narrowly conceived approach to art history, aesthetics, or measuring the relative greatness of specific works.

Now, why bring all this up? I bring it up because I love the subject matter that I have taught for some 43 years, and over those years I've gained some insight into what is behind it, where it comes from, and how it enriches human life. And I perceive that it is under various assaults today, sometimes subtle, but increasingly overt, from forces both within the traditions of which we are a part and from without them. The same elements that captured Constantinople in 1453 and destroyed the priceless mosaics of Hagia Sophia, that assaulted Vienna in 1683 (an assault thankfully repelled), that ravaged the Mediterranean world throughout the Renaissance centuries, that caused Thomas Jefferson to dispatch the Marine Corps to destroy the Barbary pirates in the 18th century, which exploded into dust the historic, monumental Buddhist sculptures along the ancient Silk Road in Afghanistan, are still very much with us. And we see their work, even now as they confidently pronounce, as if already accomplished, their supercession of a despised West, most notably in a cowering Holland, an intimidated Denmark, a listless, culturally confused Britain, and a general European population that has, if demographic projections are accurate, given up on the task of creating its own future generations. Secular Europe, freed from the dominion of Christian theology, may be having a lot of sex, even good sex at that, but not very many folks there really want to bother with children. Another popular saying comes to mind: *demography is destiny.* When I was a young man, we listened to a popular song that became a kind of hymn of the then nascent Environmentalist movement —"Where Have All The Flowers Gone?" Europeans today, the French French, the German Germans, the Italian Italians, the Danish Danes, etc. etc. might do well to contemplate a similar question: "where have all the children gone?" Well, they are there, amidst the ageing populations of those whose cultural inheritance we have peeped in on over the course of the semester. But the new, growing, and younger populations owe no allegiance to, nor have any affection for, the visions that created a Chartres Cathedral, a Sistine Ceiling, the oratorios of Bach and Handel, or, for that matter, the popular music of Broadway theatre.

So, young people today living in the West, within its context of individual liberty, freedom of expression and the artistic heritage of which we have glimpsed in this course, have something to think about, beyond all of the immediate goals of educational practice (what kind of job will I get, how much money will I make, what should I major in, etc.). Given the fact (and it is a fact, pure and simple) that there are very powerful forces, rooted in both religious fanaticism and secular, totalitarian ideology, that seek the destruction of the West and the overwhelming of its very foundations, what will things be like should they win?

This question first occurred to me in 2003, at a time when the memory of 9/11 was still vivid for most people, standing in the great long room in the library of Trinity College in Dublin. I was looking at all those books and manuscripts, ancient, medieval, and more recent, stacked floor to high ceiling, and wondered: what will happen to *this* should they win?

Stand in the Sistine Chapel and contemplate the whitewash over the mosaics of Hagia Sophia following the Ottoman conquest in 1453 and ask that question, and you might catch a glimpse of the answer. Or stand in the nave of the Paris Notre Dame Cathedral and contemplate the intentions, briefly embraced by French revolutionaries, the minions of a radical and totalitarian secularism, to raze it to the ground, and ask the question. Contemplate the astonishing fact that a passionate defense of Western Civilization by an Italian journalist, Orianna Fallaci, could result in her indictment by an Italian and a French court early in the 21st century. For writing a book. This, in the "free" world.

What these admittedly sobering thoughts suggest is that you cannot live in the world as an intellectually alive human being without holding in your thought life *the issue of destiny*, and that contemplation leads one necessarily to the now seemingly quaint, "old fashioned" concerns over the nature of Truth. We don't speak of it much nowadays, although it seemed more in view when I started teaching in 1965, so I can remember it as an energizing issue, but it has given way over the years to the more "relevant" concerns for "information" and its "processing."

Perhaps it is that shift that underlies a lament I heard recently from a vibrant, energetic, good natured and obviously fun-loving student, to the effect that "our generation" is consumed with triviality, "bullshit," and "bad music." Another memory brings me back to Venice's church of Santa Maria del Frari, in which a student, looking quietly around the environment of that sacred space, asked me "how is it that these people, with their limitations in knowledge and technology, put up such places as this, yet we today build such junk?" That was a very perceptive and passionate question, and I did not, at the time, offer an answer, but I posed a clue. It has to do with "outlook," concepts of reality, spiritual vision, or what is often identified as "worldview." Another way of looking at it is to consider the oft-stated insight that *ideas have consequences.* The question, for society, is whether the *product,* or *heritage* flowing from a stream of foundational ideas can be sustained once the grounding of those ideas is eroded through fear, rejection, or fashionable denial.

Maybe the students quoted above overstate the case, but we could consider that if their judgments are true, maybe that is because there has been no great conflict, no great truth or great falsehood holding enough power in life to fuel a greatness of imagination. Indeed, I have come to believe that the greatness of the Renaissance culture, should we assess it as such, was to a significant degree fueled by the day-to-day dangers posed to it by great civilizational forces that stood against it and sought its destruction. It is so very interesting to realize that that world which achieved so much was constantly threatened by terribly powerful forces that sought its ruin, and that indeed lived in the shock of seeing the greatest city of all Christendom sacked and brought under the control of the Muslim Ottoman empire, an event that would have been, for that world, many, many, and many times more traumatic than 9/11 was for ours. Yet, in the midst of that shattering danger, Michelangelo sculpted, Raphael painted, the papacy began to build the greatest basilica in the world, and countless other artists and craftsmen fashioned with high ambition and mind-boggling skill those great works we still celebrate, and with the pointed intention that they would last through the world's time.

Perhaps the students mentioned previously sense, at the deeper roots of being, a world of today that confirms the worst fears of the great prophet of "post-Christian" civilization, Friedrich Nietzsche, who boldly declared the "death of God" during the last decades of the 19th century, celebrating Europe's emergent freedom from theology. Yet, Nietzsche was uncertain as to what that new freedom might portend. Would it bring forth the prophesied übermensch (the Superman) or would European humanity sink instead into triviality? David Bentley Hart, of Providence College, writes of Nietzsche's uncertainty, in the context of citing the character of a world revolving around television, shopping, celebrity, and internet shallowness:

> "When one looks, for instance, at the crepuscular wasteland of modern Europe—with its aging millions milling among the glorious remnants of an artistic and architectural legacy that no modern people could hope to rival, acting out the hideously prolonged satyr play at the end of the tragic cycle of European history—it is hard to suppress a feeling of morbid despair. This was Nietzsche's greatest fear: the loss of any transcendent aspiration that could coax mighty works of cultural imagination out of a people. When the aspiring ape ceases to think himself a fallen angel, perhaps he will inevitably resign himself to being an ape, and then become contented with his lot, and ultimately even rejoice that the universe demands little more from him than an ape's contentment. If nothing else, it seems certain that post-Christian civilization will always lack the spiritual resources, or the organizing myth, necessary to produce anything

like the cultural wonders that sprang up under the sheltering canopy of the religion of the God-man." (*Atheist Delusions,* 230-231)

Andrew Leigh, in a review of the 2009 film adaptation of the Dan Brown novel *Angels and Demons,* comments similarly: *"Do you ever wonder why most modern and post-modern art and architecture seem so empty and cold, even alienating? Do you ever wonder why the art and buildings preceding the rise of Modernism are so much more inspiring than what has come since?Perhaps it's because contemporary art and architecture are the products of a culture that has rejected sanctity, eschewed sacredness."* ("Angels, Demons, and the Magical Missing Middle Easterner," at http://bighollywood.breitbart.com/aleigh/2009/05/22/)

Another writer, George Weigel, pointedly observes that *"it is fairly obvious that there is some direct, indissoluble bond between faith and the will to a future, or between the desire for a future and the imagination of eternity. . . . This is why...Europe [today] seems to lack not only the moral and imaginative resources for sustaining its civilization, but even any good reason for continuing to reproduce."* (*The Cube and the Cathedral,* 163)

The future will unfold as it will, and you will certainly see more of it than I will. And I don't want to sound despairing. I do intend, though, to pose these questions and awaken you to consider that there is a kind of glassy-eyed assumption underlying the emphases in education today that the world is sort of "set" in a default arrangement which gives us luxury to pound away at the faults in our own traditions to the point of intellectual fashion while maintaining every confidence that the things we like (freedom of expression, the wonderful places to see on holiday or interterm trips) will always be there for us. Are we in a situation where our "prophetic critique" of our own, western civilization, dims our eyes to its greatness?

There is always the possibility that we will yet see some

modern-day prophet charging forth with a vision of renewal and revivify a civilization that has laid the groundwork for all our notions of human rights, individual liberty, created the greatest and most noble narrative artforms the world has seen or is likely to ever see, and developed the recognition that even the person of the most humble origin can rise to the highest pinnacles of excellence, undergirded by a recognition that time and death are not, in fact, ultimate realities. We might well look for such a one.

But this leads me to a concluding meditation. Why is it that some things endure, and are valued even beyond the time when we have cast aside the whole basis of their origins or have dismissed the legitimacy of their substance and subject matter? (And I am not now speaking merely of things peculiar to our own tradition) Is it merely a matter of cultural bias, or the practical tasks of keeping the tourist trade viable? What is that quality of "greatness" that seems to reside, luminously and self-evidently, within things (a question that I have alluded to from time to time over the course of the semester)? Perhaps it is all just a matter of majority opinion, nothing more. But maybe not. Maybe it is more. I would suggest that it is worth considering that there is something in the processes of human labor and creativity in art, literature, music, myth, etc. that touches upon, embraces, and embodies realities (yes, *realities*) that Russell Kirk characterized as "the permanent things," or which Yale scholar Franklin Baumer identified as the "perennial issues." These are the realities that span multiculturalist divisions, and reveal a common humanity, that reveal the nature of all truly profound things, that they invite in their simplicity the meditations of the most humble intellect and yet, at the same time, open to the depths of understanding that can challenge the perception of even the greatest minds.

Although it is something of a cliché to say so, we do ignore these things and these questions at our peril, a peril to our minds, individually, and our societies, collectively. Your experiences here at college constitute an introduction to the great and universal questions, and in a real sense it matters not so much that you remember all the specifics of what you've studied, in this class or others, but more to the point is you grasp why the issues and subjects are vital to a rewarding life. The hope of the professor is always that you will go deeper in, that you won't merely cash it all in at the reception of a grade. But I am smart enough to know, too, that that issue presses with urgency upon you, so I will let you go now and prepare for Monday morning's final.

ABOUT THE AUTHOR

Richard Terrell was raised in the Chicago suburb of Bellwood, graduating from Proviso Township High School in 1958. He attended college at Illinois Wesleyan University, Bloomington, Illinois (BFA 1962) and the University of Wisconsin, Madison (MFA 1964). After a brief stint in retailing at a Chicago area department store, he assumed a teaching position at Blackburn College, Carlinville, Illinois, where he taught studio art and art history (1965-1970) and served as chair of the Humanities Division. In 1970 he accepted the position in the art department of Doane College, Crete, Nebraska, which he held until retirement in the Spring of 2009. At Doane, he taught various courses in studio art and art history, served as division chair for Fine Arts and Humanities, and taught an interdisciplinary course of his own design, entitled "Worldviews." He also pursued theological and biblical studies at Trinity Evangelical Divinity School, Deerfield, Illinois.

Mr. Terrell's essays and commentaries on the relationships between the arts and religion have been presented at various professional conferences, and in periodicals including *Christianity Today, USA Today Magazine, Eternity Magazine, Christianity and the Arts,* and *Religion and Society Journal.* In 1994, his book *Resurrecting The Third Reich,* a study of the spiritual roots of Nazism, was published by Huntington House (Lafayette, La.).

He resides in Lincoln, Nebraska with his wife, Louise, and maintains a studio at the Burkholder Project in Lincoln's Historic Haymarket District. The Terrell's have one son, a daughter, and one grand daughter who entered college in Fall, 2009.